Practice Test for the Cognitive Abilities Test (CogAT®*) Level D

Practice Test 2

By Mercer Publishing

Practice Test for the

Cognitive Abilities Test (CogAT®*) Level D

Practice Test 2

A study aid to help your child get into a gifted program.

Mercer Publishing

INTRODUCTION

As a parent and educator, I understand how important it is to ensure your children are given the opportunities they deserve when it comes to their education. One of the greatest opportunities your child will have is entering the gifted program, if they can qualify for the program based on their test scores.

One of the primary tools for measuring a student's ability to enter the gifted program is the Cognitive Abilities Test (CogAT®*) published by Riverside Publishing. This test is made up of tests in three areas: Verbal, Quantitative and Nonverbal. Your child's score on this test is likely the sole predictor of their inclusion, or non-inclusion, into the gifted program.

Most resources state that there are really no ways to prepare for this test - that your child should only get a good night's sleep before taking the test. An official practice test with sample questions does exist, but it is only available to licensed test administrators. It is guaranteed that if your child is not familiar with some of the symbols used in the test or if they have never done some of the types of problems before, that they will not do as well as they could on this test – perhaps jeopardizing their admission into the gifted program. So what should the average parent do?

If you have purchased this practice test, you have taken the first step. This practice test contains nine subtests in the three test areas found on the CogAT®* Multilevel Edition Level D exam, which is usually given to students in fifth grade**:

VERBAL

Verbal Classification	20 questions
Sentence Completion	20 questions
Verbal Analogies	25 questions

QUANTITATIVE

Quantitative Relations	25 questions
Number Series	20 questions
Equation Building	15 questions

NONVERBAL

Figure Classification	25 questions
Figure Analogies	25 questions
Figure Analysis	15 questions

The object of this practice test is to familiarize your child with the types of questions they will face on test day, how the tests are formatted, the symbols used and the number of questions in in each test area. However, since this practice test has not been standardized with Riverside Publishing and the actual CogAT®* exam, a valid CogAT®* test score cannot be concluded from their results on this practice test.

Good luck on this practice test and your upcoming gifted program exam.

Mercer Publishing

* CogAT® is a registered trademark of Houghton Mifflin Company, which was not involved in the production of, and does not endorse, this practice test.

** Based on the exam publisher's recommendation for testing gifted students. We cannot guarantee which level will be given by your school.

TABLE OF CONTENTS

TEST TAKING INFORMATION   1

VERBAL
VERBAL CLASSIFICATION   3
SENTENCE COMPLETION   6
VERBAL ANALOGIES   9

QUANTITATIVE
QUANTITATIVE RELATIONS   13
NUMBER SERIES   17
EQUATION BUILDING   20

NON-VERBAL
FIGURE CLASSIFICATION   23
FIGURE ANALOGIES   28
FIGURE ANALYSIS   33

ANSWERS   43

APPENDIX A: BUBBLE TEST FORM   53

TEST TAKING INFORMATION

The Cognitive Abilities Test (CogAT®*) Level D exam, which is usually given to students in fifth grade**, is a timed, multiple choice test. The test is self-administered, where the student reads and answers the questions themselves. Most testing for the CogAT®* Level D exam is done using electronically scored answer sheets, although answering in hand-scored booklets is sometimes also done.

The official guideline from the publisher is that students should not guess if they do not know the answer – that random guessing compromises the validity of the scores. However, the CogAT®* score is calculated based on the number of right answers and the student is not penalized for incorrect answers. As a parent looking for a high score, it is better for your child to answer all questions than leave an answer blank.

There are some approaches to standardized testing that have been proven to increase test scores. Review the following strategies with your child and have them practice these as they go through the practice test.

Listen Carefully. Instructions will be given to your child during the exam, including directions for each section and how to fill out the test forms. Many errors are made because children do not listen to the instructions as carefully as they should. If your child fills in the answers incorrectly or marks in the wrong section, your child's score will be lowered significantly.

Read the Entire Question. Some children begin filling in answers before they finish reading the entire question. It could be that the last part of the question has the information needed to answer the question correctly.

Look at all the Available Answers. In their desire to finish quickly or first, many children select the first answer that seems right to them without reading all of the answers and choosing the one that best answers the question. No additional points are given for finishing the test early. Make sure your child understands the importance of evaluating all the answers before choosing one.

Skip Difficult Questions – Return to Them Later. Many children will sit and worry about a hard question, spending so much time on one problem that they never get to problems that they would be able to answer correctly if they only had enough time. Explain to your child that they can always return to a difficult question once they finish the test section.

Eliminate Answer Choices. If your child can eliminate one or more of the answer choices as definitely wrong, their chances of guessing correctly among the remaining choices improve their odds of getting the answer right.

Practice Filling Out a Bubble Test Form. Many errors are made on the CogAT®* exam because the students do not know how to fill out a bubble test form. A sample test form has been included in Appendix A. Have your child practice filling in answers in the bubbles in the sample form so they will know what to expect on the exam day.

Now, on to the practice test.

VERBAL CLASSIFICATION

Each question in this section contains three words in bold letters. Review these words and determine why they are similar. Select the word from the five available answers that is most similar to the bold words.

20 questions
Approximate time to complete: 10 minutes

1. **bicycle   truck   van**

    A. canoe   B. vehicle   C. raft   D. drive   E. car

2. **journey   travel   trek**

    A. adjourn   B. encourage C. passive   D. migrate   E. ancestor

3. **circle   square   triangle**

    A. capital   B. cube   C. sphere   D. diamond   E. can

4. **guitar   piano   drum**

    A. microphone B. music   C. longhorn   D. trumpet   E. instrument

5. **splendid   fantastic   excellent**

    A. large   B. wonderful C. better   D. fair   E. substandard

6. **kitchen   bedroom   bathroom**

    A. house   B. den   C. landscape D. furniture   E. root

7. **flock   gather   congregate**

    A. meet   B. sermon   C. public   D. dwell   E. colonize

8. **cable   ribbon   line**

    A. chorus   B. cord   C. link   D. crop   E. quartet

9. **topic   theme   summary**

    A. report   B. subject   C. project   D. assignment   E. sentence

10. **after   since   till**

    A. time   B. behind   C. before   D. never   E. among

11. **group   tribe   clan**

    A. mother   B. tend   C. family   D. list   E. plan

12. **whale   fish   shark**

    A. rabbit   B. horse   C. seahorse   D. shell   E. ocean

13. **concert   show   performance**

    A. piano   B. conductor   C. recital   D. aisle   E. audience

14. **builder   cashier   author**

    A. career   B. skill   C. group   D. ground   E. detective

15. **they   us   them**

    A. I   B. it   C. he   D. you   E. we

16. **upon   above   on**

    A. over   B. stretch   C. after   D. below   E. across

17. **unidentified   unknown   secret**

    A. anonymous B. unanimous C. undisputed D. obvious   E. plain

18. **stitch   hem   darn**

    A. cease   B. clothe   C. sew   D. weave   E. untie

19. **me   you   her**

    A. they   B. him   C. we   D. she   E. I

20. **secure   protected   guarded**

    A. safe   B. danger   C. shelter   D. vulnerable E. saved

SENTENCE COMPLETION

Each sentence in this section is missing a word. Select the word from the five available answers that best completes the sentence.

20 questions
Approximate time to complete: 10 minutes

1.   **She put the mop and_____ back in the broom closet.**

    A. shovel   B. brush   C. tool   D. pail   E. rake

2.   **He took an _____ out in the paper to sell his car.**

    A. ad   B. stand   C. article   D. editor   E. assignment

3.   **He jumped off the diving board and _____ into the pool.**

    A. swam   B. skipped   C. glanced   D. plunged   E. reflected

4.   **Sally had to _____ her school picture since the first one had her eyes closed.**

    A. imagine   B. retake   C. visit   D. redraw   E. remind

5.   **Go three miles down this _____ and you'll see the store on your right.**

    A. hall   B. road   C. pond   D. drain   E. forest

6.   **_____ your name on the sign in sheet so that we know you are here.**

    A. Pen   B. See   C. Write   D. Make   E. Draw

7. They were _____ by the loud explosion.

   A. startled   B. suspended   C. detonated   D. quiet   E. starry

8. The two brothers _____ and disagree about everything.

   A. believe   B. agree   C. study   D. relate   E. argue

9. The _____ store sold wedding dresses.

   A. craft   B. antique   C. fabric   D. franchise   E. bridal

10. He ran so hard that he got a _____ in his side.

    A. belt   B. rib   C. pain   D. race   E. trophy

11. I would like to _____ this sweater for a smaller one.

    A. iron   B. wear   C. knit   D. exchange   E. reduce

12. The loudspeaker only _____ the argument.

    A. satisfied   B. amplified   C. encouraged   D. appointed   E. disputed

13. To make a profit, you must sell an item for _____ than it cost.

    A. fewer   B. further   C. more   D. money   E. less

14. **Our family is on a tight _____ this month so we can't afford to go to the movies.**

    A. receipt   B. rope   C. bill   D. budget   E. estate

15. **Suzie got the lead _____ in the school play.**

    A. teacher   B. role   C. curtain   D. pencil   E. stage

16. **The only place I have seen a _____ is at the zoo.**

    A. dinosaur B. cow   C. bear   D. dog   E. dragon

17. **The teacher made sure to _____ the children's names correctly on the second day of school.**

    A. pronoun   B. rapport   C. reverb   D. author   E. pronounce

18. **To get the role in the movie, more than a thousand people came to _____ .**

    A. observe   B. assemble   C. audition   D. complete   E. unite

19. **Tammy climbed aboard the _____ .**

    A. bike   B. car   C. raft   D. line   E. project

20. **When the teacher saw the students were _____ , she repeated the instructions.**

    A. exhausted B. deaf   C. confused   D. concluded E. ambitious

VERBAL ANALOGIES

Each question in this section contains three words in bold letters. Review the first two words and determine how they are related. Select the word from the five available answers that has the same relationship with the third word.

25 questions
Approximate time to complete: 10 minutes

1. **float ⟶ sink : dark ⟶**

   A. boat   B. late   C. night   D. light   E. crash

2. **wheels ⟶ bicycle : tires ⟶**

   A. tricycle   B. skateboard   C. driver   D. car   E. wheelbarrow

3. **dig ⟶ shovel : eat ⟶**

   A. food   B. meal   C. scoop   D. fork   E. cup

4. **jump ⟶ vault : jog ⟶**

   A. train   B. trot   C. compete   D. sprint   E. run

5. **tablecloth ⟶ table : sheet ⟶**

   A. paper   B. bed   C. ghost   D. piece   E. placemat

6. **miniature ⟶ small : giant ⟶**

   A. masculine   B. minuscule   C. massive   D. metaphor   E. miserly

7. **aloud** ⟶ **allowed : sea** ⟶

    A. water   B. see   C. ocean   D. river   E. marine

8. **small** ⟶ **tiny : large** ⟶

    A. big   B. giant   C. wide   D. little   E. more

9. **Germany** ⟶ **Europe : Brazil** ⟶

    A. America B. Australia C. Europe   D. Argentina E. South America

10. **good** ⟶ **unpleasant : faulty** ⟶

    A. broken   B. fine   C. defective D. confused E. incorrect

11. **grandmother** ⟶ **mother : father** ⟶

    A. grandfather B. uncle   C. boy   D. son   E. daughter

12. **word** ⟶ **sentence : sentence** ⟶

    A. letter   B. word   C. paragraph D. write   E. pen

13. **hasty** ⟶ **gradual : minor** ⟶

    A. insignificant B. elevated C. difficult D. crucial E. effortless

14. **graceful** ⟶ **agile : obvious** ⟶

   A. complex   B. apparent   C. vague   D. filtered   E. slight

15. **money** ⟶ **bank : books** ⟶

   A. learn   B. read   C. library   D. store   E. cabinet

16. **series** ⟶ **single : crowd** ⟶

   A. mob   B. individual   C. pack   D. audience   E. people

17. **careless** ⟶ **accident : trip** ⟶

   A. vacation   B. journey   C. spree   D. slip   E. fall

18. **adorn** ⟶ **embellish : perish** ⟶

   A. survive   B. church   C. sustain   D. obtain   E. die

19. **tired** ⟶ **sleep : hungry** ⟶

   A. starve   B. drink   C. meal   D. eat   E. hunger

20. **famous** ⟶ **infamous : fib** ⟶

   A. excuse   B. represent   C. insult   D. offend   E. deception

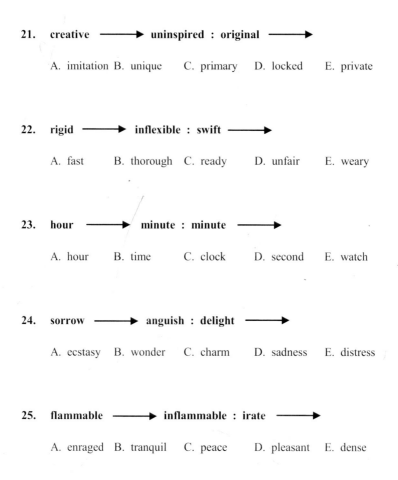

21. creative ⟶ uninspired : original ⟶

A. imitation B. unique C. primary D. locked E. private

22. rigid ⟶ inflexible : swift ⟶

A. fast B. thorough C. ready D. unfair E. weary

23. hour ⟶ minute : minute ⟶

A. hour B. time C. clock D. second E. watch

24. sorrow ⟶ anguish : delight ⟶

A. ecstasy B. wonder C. charm D. sadness E. distress

25. flammable ⟶ inflammable : irate ⟶

A. enraged B. tranquil C. peace D. pleasant E. dense

QUANTITATIVE RELATIONS

Each question in this section contains two items to compare. Review items I and II. Determine if one is greater than the other or if they are equal. Then select the answer that reflects that relationship.

25 questions
Approximate time to complete: 12 minutes

1. I. 9876
    II. 9865

    A. I is greater than II.
    B. I is less than II.
    C. I is equal to II.

2. I. 71 sq. ft.
    II. 75 sq. ft.

    A. I is greater than II.
    B. I is less than II.
    C. I is equal to II.

3. I. 3 boys + 2 girls
    II. 2 girls + 3 boys

    A. I is more people than II.
    B. I is less people than II.
    C. I is the same number of people as II.

4. I. 2 weeks
    II. 16 days

    A. I is longer than II.
    B. I is shorter than II.
    C. I is the same length of time as II.

5. I. 99.9999
    II. 100

    A. I is greater than II.
    B. I is less than II.
    C. I is equal to II.

6. I. 98 + 89
    II. 97 + 79

    A. I is greater than II.
    B. I is less than II.
    C. I is equal to II.

7.   I. 5 quarters
      II. 1.75

A. I is greater than II.
B. I is less than II.
C. I is equal to II.

8.   I. 3/4 foot
      II. 10 inches

A. I is longer than II.
B. I is shorter than II.
C. I is the same length as II.

9.   I. 353 + 22
      II. 322 + 53

A. I is greater than II.
B. I is less than II.
C. I is equal to II.

10.   I. 4 x 4 x 4
      II. 99

A. I is greater than II.
B. I is less than II.
C. I is equal to II.

11.   I. diamond
      II. parallelogram

A. I has more sides than II.
B. I has fewer sides than II.
C. I has the same number of sides as II.

12.   I. 33.3 + 66.6
      II. 100

A. I is greater than II.
B. I is less than II.
C. I is equal to II.

13.   I. 40027
      II. 39905

A. I is greater than II.
B. I is less than II.
C. I is equal to II.

14.   I. 3 weeks
      II. 30 days

A. I is longer than II.
B. I is shorter than II.
C. I is the same length of time as II.

15.   I.   200 + 800
      II.   400 + 500

A. I is greater than II.
B. I is less than II.
C. I is equal to II.

16.   I.   70.07
      II.   70.08

A. I is greater than II.
B. I is less than II.
C. I is equal to II.

17.   I.   39974
      II.   39815

A. I is greater than II.
B. I is less than II.
C. I is equal to II.

18.   I.   2/3 foot
      II.   9 inches

A. I is longer than II.
B. I is shorter than II.
C. I is the same length as II.

19.   I.   -6.6
      II.   -6.5

A. I is greater than II.
B. I is less than II.
C. I is equal to II.

20.   I.   39905
      II.   39845

A. I is greater than II.
B. I is less than II.
C. I is equal to II.

21.   I.   2 girls and a cat
      II.   2 cats and a bird

A. I has more legs than II.
B. I has fewer legs than II.
C. I has the same number of legs as II.

22.   I.   -2367
      II.   -2376

A. I is greater than II.
B. I is less than II.
C. I is equal to II.

23.   I. 5 inches   A. I is longer than II.
       II. 1/2 foot   B. I is shorter than II.
                                            C. I is the same length as II.

24.   I. 39815   A. I is greater than II.
       II. 39817   B. I is less than II.
                                            C. I is equal to II.

25.   I. -1   A. I is greater than II.
       II. 1   B. I is less than II.
                                            C. I is equal to II.

NUMBER SERIES

Each question in this section contains a series of numbers in bold. Review the numbers to determine the rule for their order. Select the number from the five available answers that should come next in the series.

20 questions
Approximate time to complete: 12 minutes

1. **9 7 9 7 9** ⟶

   A. 6   B. 8   C. 7   D. 4   E. 9

2. **8 10 13 15 18** ⟶

   A. 18   B. 19   C. 20   D. 21   E. 22

3. **19 34 49 64 79** ⟶

   A. 104   B. 82   C. 94   D. 99   E. 91

4. **69 61 53 45 37** ⟶

   A. 26   B. 30   C. 32   D. 29   E. 27

5. **6 2 3 6 2** ⟶

   A. 2   B. 4   C. 1   D. 3   E. 5

6. **19 16.5 14 11.5 9** ⟶

   A. 5.5   B. 7.5   C. 7   D. 6   E. 6.5

7. 113 105 97 89 81 ⟶

A. 72   B. 73   C. 75   D. 79   E. 77

8. 4 4 1 4 4 ⟶

A. 7   B. 1   C. 0   D. 4   E. 6

9. 4 1 5 2 6 ⟶

A. 7   B. 3   C. 2   D. 5   E. 6

10. 6.75 10 13.25 16.5 19.75 ⟶

A. 24.25   B. 23.75   C. 23   D. 23.5   E. 22.75

11. 26 76 126 176 226 ⟶

A. 276   B. 256   C. 286   D. 266   E. 176

12. 2 7 9 2 7 ⟶

A. 6   B. 7   C. 2   D. 8   E. 9

13. 165 140 115 90 65 ⟶

A. 40   B. 50   C. 15   D. 27   E. 30

14. **211 170 129 88 47** ——————▶

    A. 8   B. 6   C. 23   D. 4   E. 17

15. **5   7   6   8   7** ——————▶

    A. 8   B. 4   C. 9   D. 11   E. 5

16. **7.5 11.25 15 18.75 22.5** ——————▶

    A. 26   B. 26.75   C. 26.25   D. 27   E. 26.5

17. **18 15 11 8 4** ——————▶

    A. 0   B. 2   C. 4   D. 1   E. 3

18. **10 37 64 91 118** ——————▶

    A. 130   B. 135   C. 145   D. 140   E. 138

19. **6 8 7 9 8** ——————▶

    A. 6   B. 7   C. 9   D. 10   E. 12

20. **9 11 15 21 29** ——————▶

    A. 36   B. 37   C. 38   D. 39   E. 40

EQUATION BUILDING

Each question in this section contains a series of numbers and numerical signs in bold. Arrange and rearrange each of the numbers and signs to come up with one of the five available answers.

15 questions
Approximate time to complete: 12 minutes

1.   **3   4   5   x   +**

    A. 3   B. 22   C. 35   D. 16   E. 17

2.   **3 2 2 + -**

    A. 5   B. 1   C. 4   D. 0   E. 2

3.   **10 7 3 + +**

    A. 25   B. 10   C. 20   D. 24   E. 12

4.   **10 3 3 x -**

    A. 30   B. 10   C. 27   D. 0   E. 21

5.   **8 3 4 x +**

    A. 24   B. 8   C. 18   D. 20   E. 23

6.   **10 1 8 - -**

    A. 4   B. 10   C. 1   D. 0   E. 7

7. **9   8   5   x   -**

   A. 72   B. 0   C. 9   D. 66   E. 67

8. **7   5   4   +   -**

   A. 4   B. 7   C. 9   D. 2   E. 0

9. **9   9   5   x   +**

   A. 59   B. 9   C. 53   D. 90   E. 54

10. **2   1   10   x   x**

    A. 21   B. 11   C. 19   D. 13   E. 20

11. **9   8   8   +   -**

    A. 8   B. 10   C. 7   D. 0   E. 12

12. **10   9   6   +   -**

    A. 7   B. 12   C. 0   D. 8   E. 10

13. **10   10   7   x   +**

    A. 140   B. 80   C. 10   D. 18   E. 2

14. **10** **5** **5** **x** **-**

    A. 40   B. 0   C. 25   D. 17   E. 45

15. **7** **8** **3** **x** **x**

    A. 148   B. 53   C. 168   D. 31   E. 18

FIGURE CLASSIFICATION

Review the first three figures in each question and determine why they are similar. Select the figure from the five available answers that is most similar to the first three figures.

25 questions
Approximate time to complete: 10 minutes

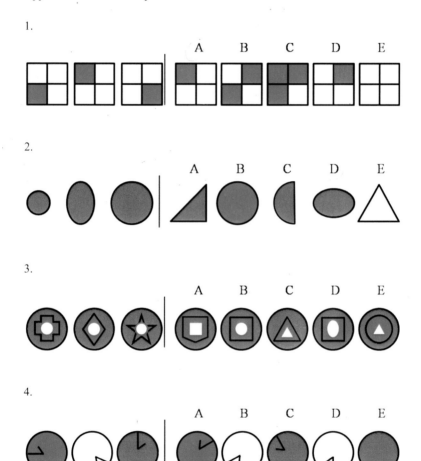

1.

2.

3.

4.

5.

                A   B   C   D   E

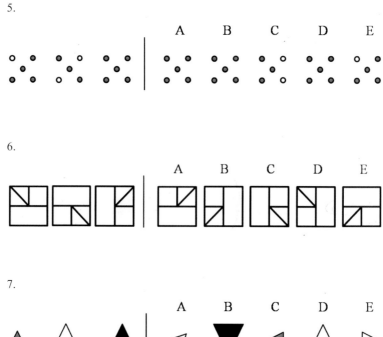

6.

                A   B   C   D   E

7.

                A   B   C   D   E

8.

                A   B   C   D   E

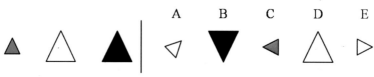

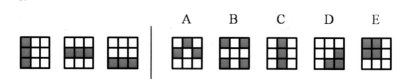

9.

                A   B   C   D   E

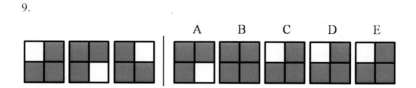

10.

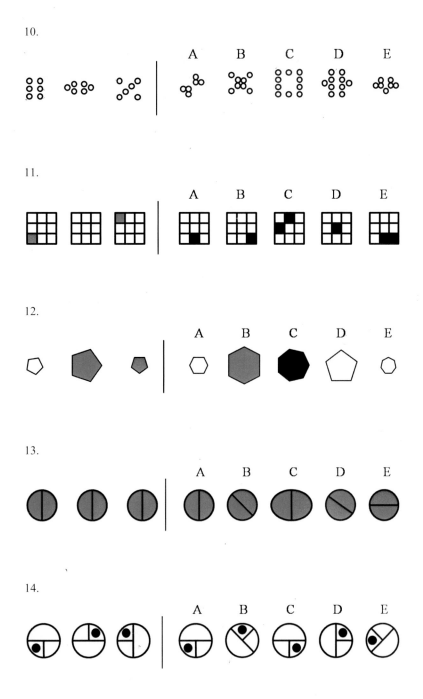

11.

12.

13.

14.

15.

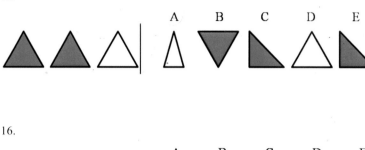

16.

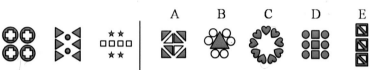

17.

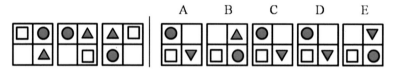

18.

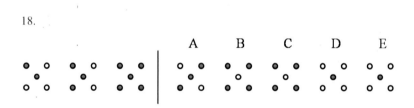

19.

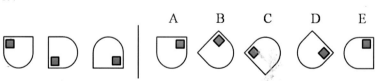

20.

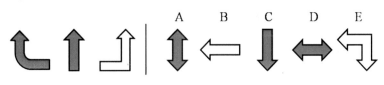

21.

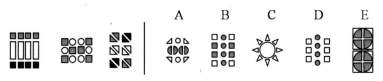

22.

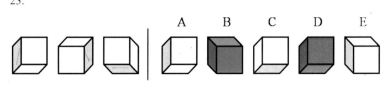

23.

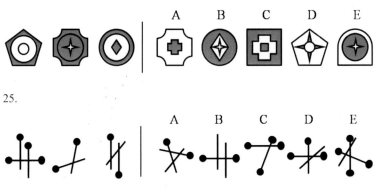

24.

25.

FIGURE ANALOGIES

Review the first two figures in each question. The first figure is modified into
the second figure in some way. Select the figure from the five available
answers that will be created when that same modification is done to the third
figure.

25 questions
Approximate time to complete: 10 minutes

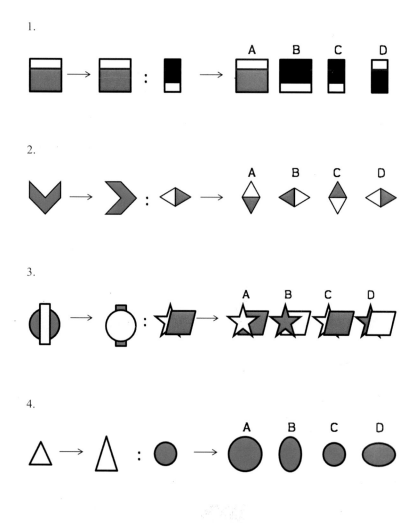

5.

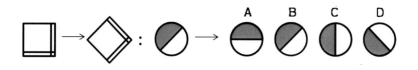

6.

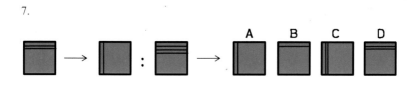

7.

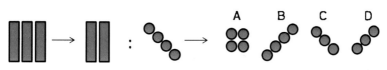

8.

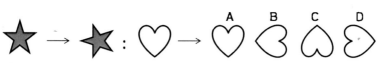

9.

10.

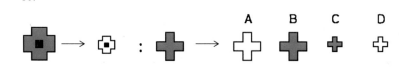

11.

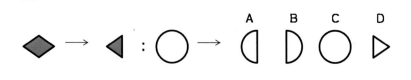

12.

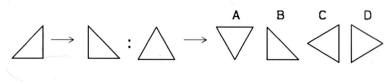

13.

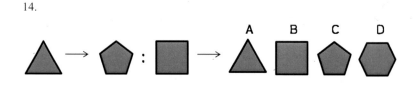

14.

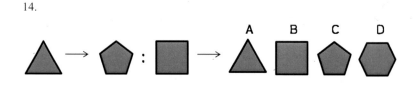

15.

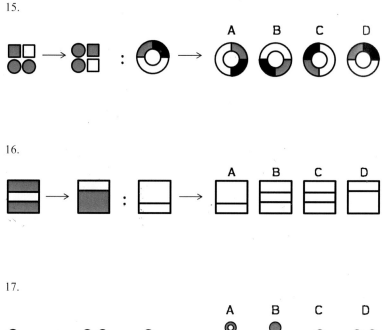

16.

17.

18.

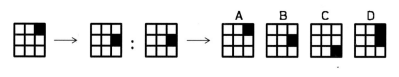

19.

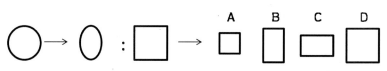

20.

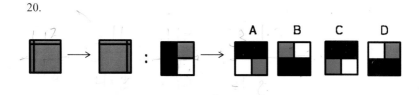

21.

22.

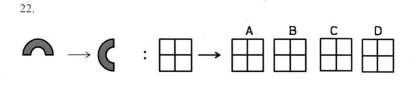

23.

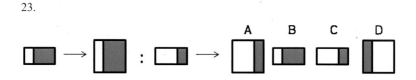

24.

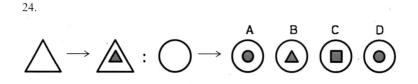

25.

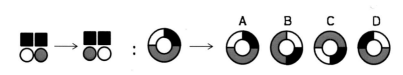

FIGURE ANALYSIS

Each question in this section shows a square piece of paper being folded and then hole-punched. Select the piece of paper from the five available answers that shows how the paper will look when it is unfolded.

15 questions
Approximate time to complete: 10 minutes

1.

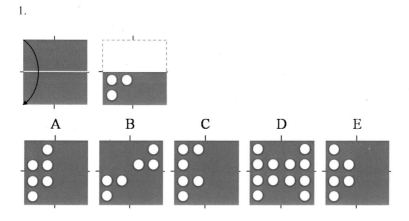

2.

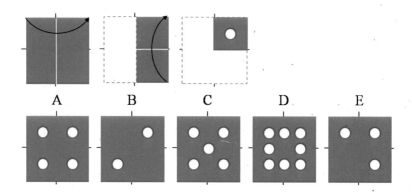

3.

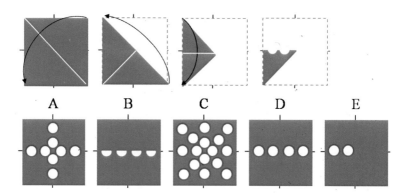

4.

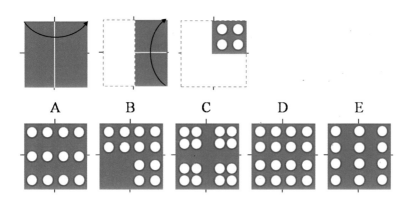

5.

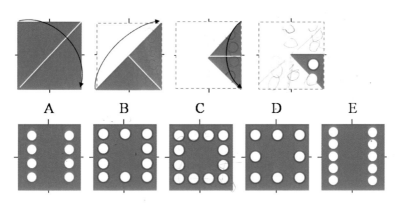

6.

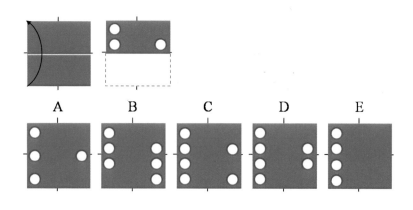

A   B   C   D   E

7.

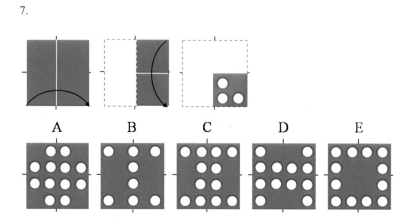

A   B   C   D   E

8.

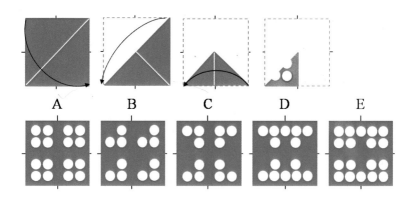

9.

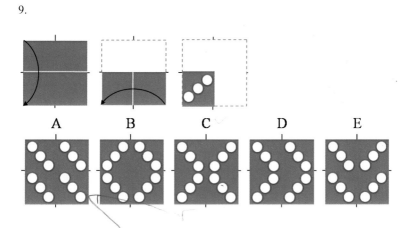

10.

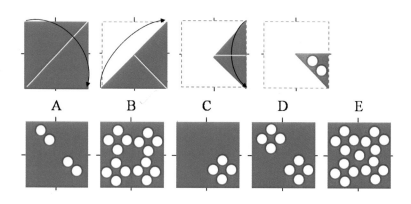

A   B   C   D   E

11.

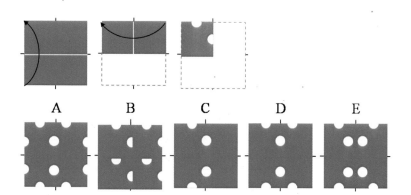

A   B   C   D   E

12.

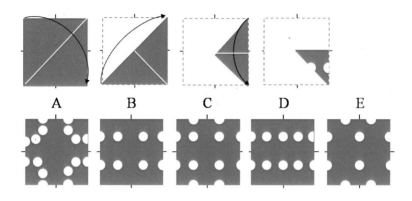

| A | B | C | D | E |

13.

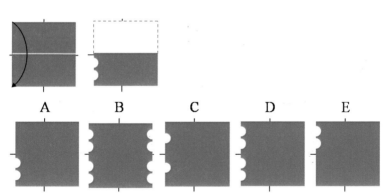

| A | B | C | D | E |

14.

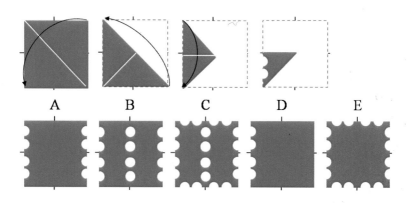

15.

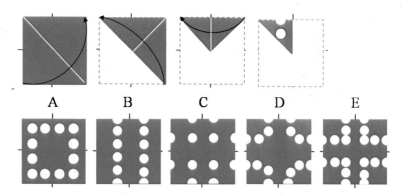

ANSWERS

VERBAL CLASSIFICATION

1. E. Vehicles/Things with Wheels
2. D. Synonyms
3. D. Two-Dimensional Shapes
4. D. Musical Instruments
5. B. Synonyms
6. B. Types of Rooms
7. A. Synonyms
8. B. Types of String/Rope
9. B. Synonyms
10. C. Prepositions Related to Time
11. C. Groups of People
12. C. Things that Swim
13. C. Synonyms
14. E. Jobs/Professions
15. E. Pronouns for more than one person
16. A. Prepositions Related to Above
17. A. Synonyms
18. C. Synonyms
19. B. Objective Pronouns
20. A. Synonyms

SENTENCE COMPLETION

1. D. pail
2. A. ad
3. D. plunged
4. B. retake
5. B. road
6. C. Write
7. A. startled
8. E. argue
9. E. bridal
10. C. pain
11. D. exchange
12. B. amplified
13. C. more
14. D. budget
15. B. role
16. C. bear
17. E. pronounce
18. C. audition
19. C. raft
20. C. confused

VERBAL ANALOGIES

1. D. Opposite
2. D. Object that is part of the whole
3. D. Object and how/where it is used
4. D. Degrees
5. B. Object and where it is located
6. C. Similar
7. B. Words That Sound the Same
8. B. Degrees
9. E. Object that is part of the whole
10. B. Opposite
11. D. Similar Relationship
12. C. Object that is part of the whole
13. D. Opposite
14. A. Similar
15. C. Object and where it is located
16. B. Groups or Part of the Group
17. E. Cause / Effect
18. E. Similar
19. C. Cause / Effect
20. E. Degrees
21. A. Opposite
22. A. Similar
23. D. Groups or Part of the Group
24. A. Degrees
25. A. Similar

QUANTITATIVE RELATIONS

1. A
2. B
3. C
4. B
5. B
6. A
7. B
8. B
9. C
10. B
11. C
12. B
13. A
14. B
15. A
16. B
17. A
18. B
19. B
20. A
21. B
22. A
23. B
24. B
25. B

NUMBER SERIES

1. C. The first two numbers are repeated.
2. C. Add 2, 3, 2, 3, 2
3. C. Add 15 each time
4. D. Subtract 8 each time
5. D. The first three numbers are repeated.
6. E. Subtract 2.5 each time
7. B. Subtract 8 each time
8. B. The first three numbers are repeated.
9. B. Add 1 to the first number to get the third number. Add 1 to the
        second number to get the fourth.
10. C. Add 3.25 each time
11. A. Add 50 each time
12. E. The first three numbers are repeated.
13. A. Subtract 25 each time
14. B. Subtract 41 each time
15. C. Add 1 to the first number to get the third number. Add 1 to the
         second number to get the fourth.
16. C. Add 3.75 each time
17. D. Subtract 3, 4, 3, 4, 3
18. C. Add 27 each time
19. D. Add 1 to the first number to get the third number. Add 1 to the
         second number to get the fourth.
20. D. Add 2, 4, 6, 8, 10

EQUATION BUILDING

1. E. 3 x 4 + 5 = 17
2. B. 2 + 2 - 3 = 1
3. C. 10 + 7 + 3 = 20
4. C. 10 x 3 - 3 = 27
5. D. 3 x 4 + 8 = 20
6. C. 10 - 1 - 8 = 1
7. E. 9 x 8 - 5 = 67
8. D. 5 + 4 - 7 = 2
9. E. 9 x 5 + 9 = 54
10. E. 2 x 1 x 10 = 20
11. C. 8 + 8 - 9 = 7
12. A. 10 + 6 - 9 = 7
13. B. 10 x 7 + 10 = 80
14. E. 10 x 5 - 5 = 45
15. C. 7 x 8 x 3 = 168

FIGURE CLASSIFICATION

1. A. Each figure has one blue square.
2. D. Each figure is red and rounded (circle or oval).
3. B. Each figure has an inner circle.
4. D. Each figure is the same only rotated.. The lines in the wrong answers are opposite.
5. C. Each figure has three blue dots.
6. B. Each figure is a rotation of the same figure.
7. D. Each figure is an unrotated triangle. Different sizes are OK.
8. C. Each figure has three red squares in a line.
9. C. Each figure is a rotation of the same figure.
10. A. Each figure has 6 circles.
11. B. Each figure has one colored corner square.
12. D. Each figure is a pentagon. Different sizes and rotations are OK.
13. A. Each figure is the same shape, without rotation.
14. A. Each figure is the same, only rotated. The black dot should be in the same location.
15. D. Each figure is an equilateral triangle with the point facing up.
16. A. Each figure has 8 shapes.
17. B. Each figure has a yellow square, a blue circle and a triangle that points up.
18. E. Each figure has a red center dot.
19. E. Each figure is the same, only rotated. The blue square should be in the same location.
20. E. Each figure is the square in the same corner relative to the angled corner.
21. B. Each figure has 12 shapes.
22. A. Each figure is an arrow that points up.
23. A. Each figure is a rotation of the same figure.
24. E. Each figure has a middle circle.
25. A. Each figure has 2 lines with a circle at one end.

FIGURE ANALOGIES

1. C. Same.
2. C. Rotate Counterclockwise.
3. B. Reverse the Order, Reverse Colors.
4. B. Enlarge Height.
5. C. Rotate 45 Degrees Counterclockwise.
6. B. Half to Whole Shape.
7. C. Remove 1 Line and Rotate Counterclockwise.
8. C. Reduce by 1.
9. D. Rotate Counterclockwise.
10. D. Reduce Size of Figure, Color Change.
11. B. Flip Horizontally.
12. A. Whole to Half Shape (Left Half).
13. D. Rotate 180 Degrees.
14. D. Add 2 Sides.
15. A. Rotate Clockwise.
16. B. Move Bar 1/3 Up.
17. D. Add 1 Horizontally.
18. C. Move Black Square 1 Down.
19. B. Reduce Width.
20. A. Rotate Clockwise.
21. A. Move Bar 1/3 Right.
22. A. Rotate Counterclockwise.
23. A. Enlarge Height.
24. D. Add Blue Inner Shape (Same Shape as Outer Shape).
25. D. Flip Horizontally.

FIGURE ANALYSIS

1. E
2. A
3. A
4. D
5. C
6. D
7. C
8. A
9. C
10. B
11. D
12. C
13. D
14. E
15. D

APPENDIX A

BUBBLE TEST FORM

Many errors are made on the CogAT®* exam because the students do not know
how to fill out a bubble test form. Have your child practice filling in answers
in the bubbles below.

1 Ⓐ Ⓑ Ⓒ Ⓓ Ⓔ		1 Ⓐ Ⓑ Ⓒ Ⓓ Ⓔ
2 Ⓐ Ⓑ Ⓒ Ⓓ Ⓔ		2 Ⓐ Ⓑ Ⓒ Ⓓ Ⓔ
3 Ⓐ Ⓑ Ⓒ Ⓓ Ⓔ		3 Ⓐ Ⓑ Ⓒ Ⓓ Ⓔ
4 Ⓐ Ⓑ Ⓒ Ⓓ Ⓔ		4 Ⓐ Ⓑ Ⓒ Ⓓ Ⓔ
5 Ⓐ Ⓑ Ⓒ Ⓓ Ⓔ		5 Ⓐ Ⓑ Ⓒ Ⓓ Ⓔ
6 Ⓐ Ⓑ Ⓒ Ⓓ Ⓔ		6 Ⓐ Ⓑ Ⓒ Ⓓ Ⓔ
7 Ⓐ Ⓑ Ⓒ Ⓓ Ⓔ		7 Ⓐ Ⓑ Ⓒ Ⓓ Ⓔ
8 Ⓐ Ⓑ Ⓒ Ⓓ Ⓔ		8 Ⓐ Ⓑ Ⓒ Ⓓ Ⓔ
9 Ⓐ Ⓑ Ⓒ Ⓓ Ⓔ		9 Ⓐ Ⓑ Ⓒ Ⓓ Ⓔ
10 Ⓐ Ⓑ Ⓒ Ⓓ Ⓔ		10 Ⓐ Ⓑ Ⓒ Ⓓ Ⓔ
11 Ⓐ Ⓑ Ⓒ Ⓓ Ⓔ		11 Ⓐ Ⓑ Ⓒ Ⓓ Ⓔ
12 Ⓐ Ⓑ Ⓒ Ⓓ Ⓔ		12 Ⓐ Ⓑ Ⓒ Ⓓ Ⓔ
13 Ⓐ Ⓑ Ⓒ Ⓓ Ⓔ		13 Ⓐ Ⓑ Ⓒ Ⓓ Ⓔ
14 Ⓐ Ⓑ Ⓒ Ⓓ Ⓔ		14 Ⓐ Ⓑ Ⓒ Ⓓ Ⓔ
15 Ⓐ Ⓑ Ⓒ Ⓓ Ⓔ		15 Ⓐ Ⓑ Ⓒ Ⓓ Ⓔ
16 Ⓐ Ⓑ Ⓒ Ⓓ Ⓔ		16 Ⓐ Ⓑ Ⓒ Ⓓ Ⓔ
17 Ⓐ Ⓑ Ⓒ Ⓓ Ⓔ		17 Ⓐ Ⓑ Ⓒ Ⓓ Ⓔ
18 Ⓐ Ⓑ Ⓒ Ⓓ Ⓔ		18 Ⓐ Ⓑ Ⓒ Ⓓ Ⓔ
19 Ⓐ Ⓑ Ⓒ Ⓓ Ⓔ		19 Ⓐ Ⓑ Ⓒ Ⓓ Ⓔ
20 Ⓐ Ⓑ Ⓒ Ⓓ Ⓔ		20 Ⓐ Ⓑ Ⓒ Ⓓ Ⓔ
21 Ⓐ Ⓑ Ⓒ Ⓓ Ⓔ		21 Ⓐ Ⓑ Ⓒ Ⓓ Ⓔ
22 Ⓐ Ⓑ Ⓒ Ⓓ Ⓔ		22 Ⓐ Ⓑ Ⓒ Ⓓ Ⓔ
23 Ⓐ Ⓑ Ⓒ Ⓓ Ⓔ		23 Ⓐ Ⓑ Ⓒ Ⓓ Ⓔ
24 Ⓐ Ⓑ Ⓒ Ⓓ Ⓔ		24 Ⓐ Ⓑ Ⓒ Ⓓ Ⓔ
25 Ⓐ Ⓑ Ⓒ Ⓓ Ⓔ		25 Ⓐ Ⓑ Ⓒ Ⓓ Ⓔ

MERCER PUBLISHING

Mercer Publishing understands how important it is to ensure your children are given the opportunities they deserve when it comes to their education. One of the greatest opportunities your child will have is entering the gifted program, if they can qualify for the program based on their test scores.

We provide practice test books for gifted program entry exams that offer:

- Similar questions and test formats to the actual tests
- Full-length practice tests
- Answer keys

These books are invaluable tools for your child to score their best - and get into the gifted program!

Please visit our website to find out the current gifted program exams that are available.